W9-AZB-126

Experiments with
STATES OF
MATTER

TREVOR COOK

PowerKiDS press

New York

Published in 2009 by The Rosen Publishing Group, Inc.
29 East 21st Street, New York, NY 10010

Editor: Alex Woolf
Designers: Sally Henry and Trevor Cook
Consultant: Keith Clayson
U.S. Editor: Kara Murray

Picture Credits: Sally Henry and Trevor Cook

Every attempt has been made to clear copyright. Should there be any
inadvertent omission, please apply to the publisher for rectification.

Library of Congress Cataloging-in-Publication Data

Cook, Trevor, 1948–
  Experiments with states of matter / Trevor Cook.
    p. cm. — (Science lab)
  Includes index.
  ISBN 978-1-4358-2805-6 (library binding) — ISBN 978-1-4358-3218-3 (pbk.)
ISBN 978-1-4042-8023-6 (6-pack)
  1. Matter—Properties—Experiments—Juvenile literature. I. Title.
  QC173.36.C66 2009
  530.4078—dc22
                              2008032711

Printed in the United States

Contents

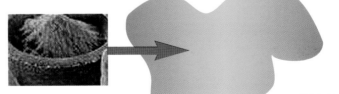

Introduction

Elements are all around and inside us. Our bodies are made up mostly of carbon, hydrogen, oxygen, nitrogen, calcium and phosphorus.

Carbon is the fourth most common element in the universe. It is also found in the form of diamonds, charcoal and pencil lead, as graphite.

This symbol is a corrosive chemical warning.

Hydrogen, a gas, is the most common element. With oxygen, it forms water as well as corrosive chemicals.

Oxygen is used in welding.

Oxygen is the third most common element and makes up 21 percent of air.

In May 1937, a famous German airship, the *Hindenburg,* burst into flames near its mooring mast in New Jersey. Hydrogen and oxygen made an explosive mixture.

78 percent of air is nitrogen. It's a gas that helps make rocket fuel, explosives and fertilizer.

We have calcium in our teeth and bones. It is a metal also found in cement and in fireworks.

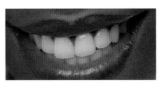

Phosphorus is a metal that explodes when exposed to air.

It's used in making fertilizers and matches.

Some technical or unusual words, shown in *italic* type, are explained in the glossary on page 31.

Materials and Tools

You should easily find many things that you need for our experiments around the house.

20 minutes

This tells you about how long a project could take.

This symbol means you might need adult help.

Jars Try to save as many different clean, empty jars at home as you can. We are going to need quite a few for the experiments. Afterwards you can recycle them.

Mixing bowl This will be necessary for several projects. Use a plastic bowl if you can.

Kettle You will sometimes need to use boiling water. Ask an adult to help. Check that the kettle or stove is turned off when you have finished with it.

Popsicle sticks These are ideal for stirring mixtures or lighting tea lights. Collect them next time you eat popsicles!

Matches Always be very careful with matches. Ask an adult to help you. Extra long matches would be very useful in some of our experiments.

Tongs They are useful for gripping hot things.

Plastic dropper You can get one at an arts and crafts shop, ideal for controlling drops of liquid.

Tea light Small candles with a metal case, tea lights are safer and more stable than candles. Be sure to handle with care. Never leave lighted tea lights unattended.

Scissors Use safety scissors that you can keep for all your science experiments. Keep them away from young children.

Kitchen supplies Be careful when using food or anything from unmarked bottles. Check with an adult and get permission first.

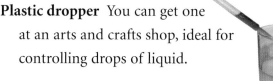

Funnel It is very useful for filtering liquids when used with filter paper or paper towels. It is also handy for filling bottles.

Baking tray A metal tray, usually used in the oven, will be very useful to you for the volcano project, as it could get a bit messy!

Saucepan Ask an adult to find an old saucepan you can use, especially for the colored dye experiments!

String Ordinary household string will be fine for most of our needs.

Balloons Next time you have a party, keep a few balloons for use in our balancing experiment! (see page 28)

Notebook
Keep a special notebook to record the results of your experiments.

Colored markers
You will find it handy to have a box of *water-soluble* colored markers for several of the projects. For the chromatography experiment on page 16, you will need to use at least six different colors.

Friends can help
Do the experiments with your friends when you can, especially when you can wow them with magic! (see page 30)

Growing Crystals

A crystal is a solid that forms itself into a very regular three-dimensional pattern. Crystals are formed when a liquid cools and turns into a solid. The arrangement of *atoms* in the solid produces the shape of the crystal.

An example of this is when water is cooled and becomes ice.

You will need:

- sugar, glass jar
- coarse string, a popsicle stick
- hot water, spoon
- salt, sand, soil
- 2 jars, plastic bag
- coffee filter or paper towel
- funnel and a small plate

The plan

We are going to *dissolve* some ingredients in water. We will try to grow crystals. Then we will use crystallization to purify salt.

Experiment 1

water level

end of string

1 Put some hot water into a jar. Water from the hot tap should be hot enough.

2 Add sugar, one spoonful at a time, using the popsicle stick as a stirrer. Keep adding more sugar until you can't dissolve any more. You will see undissolved sugar left at the bottom of the jar.

3 Tie the string to the popsicle stick, hang it in the sugar solution and leave to cool. The string is a good surface for growing crystals.

4 As the solution cools, crystals begin to form on the string. Be patient, it can take a few days for crystals to form, provided you have made a saturated solution.

What's going on?

The sugar dissolves in water to form a sugar solution. Hot water allows more sugar to dissolve. As the water cools, it cannot hold as much sugar in solution, and some sugar changes back to a solid.

What else can you do?

Try different kinds of sugar! Use light or dark brown sugar. Check for it in your kitchen cabinet.

Experiment 2

1 Mix salt, soil and sand together thoroughly with a spoon on a piece of plastic bag.

2 Stir the mixture into warm water and leave to settle overnight.

3 Pour the liquid through a filter, being careful to leave the sediment in the bottom of the jar. Leave the filtered liquid on the plate in a warm place.

What's going on?

Only the salt dissolves in the water. Letting the solution stand allows the heavier particles of sand and soil to be pulled to the bottom of the jar by gravity. Filtering removes the smaller sand and soil particles. Finally, on the plate, the water *evaporates* to leave just the salt crystals.

Acids and Bases

All liquids are either acidic, *neutral* or *basic*. Examples of acids are acetic acid (in vinegar) and citric acid (in oranges and lemons). Strong acids can eat away metal. Very strong *bases* can cause chemical burns.

You will need:

- knife for chopping, 2 glasses
- heat-resistant bowls or jars, kettle
- household chemicals
- plastic dropper
- red cabbage

The plan

We are going to make an *indicator* that will tell us which liquids are acidic and which are basic.

What to do:

1 Ask an adult to chop into small pieces about two cups of cabbage. Place them in the bowl.

2 Pour some boiling water onto the red cabbage and leave for 15 minutes. Ask an adult to pour the water.

3 Pour off the liquid into a bowl. This liquid is our indicator.

4 You need two liquids to test your indicator. We are using white vinegar (acid) and a solution of baking soda in water (base).

5 Add indicator to each liquid in drops. Watch the color change. Wash the glasses thoroughly between tests.

6 See where the results fall on this chart.

◄ more acidic		neutral		more alkaline ►
red	purple	blue-violet	blue-green	green-yellow

What else can you do?

Try other kinds of colored vegetable juice to see if they make indicators.

What's going on?

The *pigments* from the cabbage react with acids and bases to change the color. The juice should turn pink in acidic solutions and green in basic ones.

Put some indicator drops in plain water. This is your neutral color. Use your indicator to test other liquids and compare the results.

Jargon Buster
Acids are found in citrus fruits.
Bases are found in soap.

Color Storm

Oil and water don't mix. Or do they? Here we show in a very colorful way the difference a little dishwashing liquid can make.

You will need:

- 2 white plates or saucers
- full fat milk
- dishwashing liquid
- matchstick or skewer
- 3 or 4 colors of food coloring
- notebook and pencil

The plan

We are going to add food coloring to water and then to milk. Then we'll see what happens when we drop dishwashing liquid into the mixtures.

1 Pour water onto a saucer or plate. Wait for a minute or so until the water stops moving.

2 Put some evenly spaced drops of food coloring in the water.

3 Pour some milk onto the other saucer or plate. Wait for a minute for the milk to stop moving.

4 Put some drops of food coloring in the milk, evenly spaced.

5 Add one drop of dishwashing liquid to each of the saucers.

6 Look at your saucers after a few minutes, then again after 10 minutes.

7 Look at your saucers again after 20 minutes. Use a notepad and pencil to write down the results.

Make notes of what you see:

- What happens when you add the food coloring to the water?
- What happens when you add the coloring to the milk?
- What happens when you add the dishwashing liquid to the water and milk?
- Read on to find out why these things happen.

What's going on?

Milk is a special mixture of fat and water called an emulsion. The fat is not dissolved in the water, but the two are mixed together. (If your milk has cream on the surface, that is because some of the fat has separated and floated to the top.)

The food coloring doesn't travel through milk as readily as it does through water because it mixes with only the watery part of the milk. When you add dishwashing liquid, two things happen – the surface tension of the water is *destroyed*, and the fat and water start to mix together because the dishwashing liquid breaks up the fat.

The movement of the food coloring shows you what's happening. It moves to the side of the saucer when the surface tension is broken, and it swirls in patterns as the fat and water mix together.

What else can you do?

Try using a saucer of vegetable oil. What do you think will happen? Try not to spill the oil, as it can be hard to clean and it can stain things. Try other different liquids, or liquids at different temperatures.

Jargon Buster
Food coloring is harmless, but it will stain your hands and clothes.

Chromatography

Chromatography is a technique for separating and identifying the parts that make up a mixture.

The plan

We are going to use one type of chromatography, called paper chromatography, to find out what pigments make up different colored inks.

You will need:

- colored felt-tip markers (not *permanent* or *waterproof*)
- blotting paper
- ruler, scissors
- tape, bowl, water
- pencil, notebook

What to do:

1 Cut blotting paper into strips, 4 x .5 inches (100 x 15 mm).

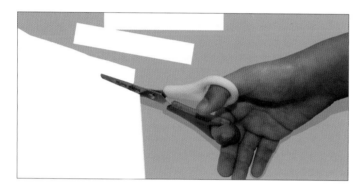

2 Number the strips and tape them to the ruler.

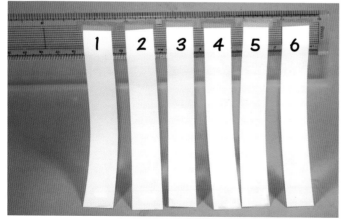

3 Put a small dot of different color on each strip, noting each strip number as the color is put on.

16

4 Fill the bowl half full with water. Hang the strips over the edge of the bowl, so that the ends are just touching the water.

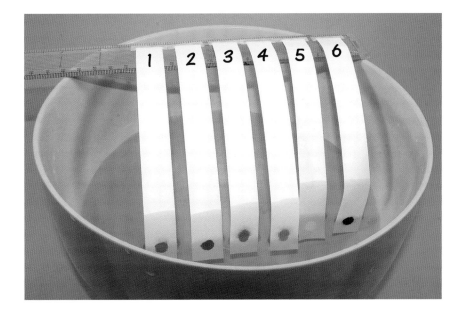

5 Wait until the water is ¾ inch (20 mm) or so from the ruler, then remove the strips from the bowl and record the colors you see. Sometimes a black will give you a very surprising result!

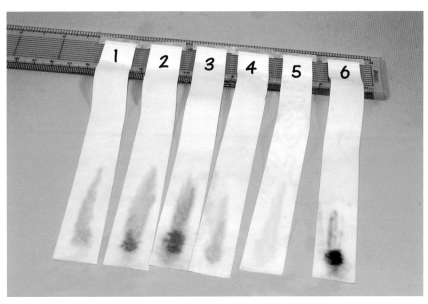

What's going on?

Water moves up the strips by capillary action and carries the pigments with it. Some pigments are more strongly attracted to the paper fibers and so are not carried as far. A color may be made of many different pigments.

What else can you do?

Try using other colored substances, such as food dye.

Jargon Buster
Capillary action is the way a liquid such as water is drawn into tiny spaces in a material by the attraction between molecules.

Oxygen and Burning

One of the *components* of air is oxygen. Without it we would not be able to breathe and nothing would burn!

You will need:

- jar with lid, thread spool
- tea lights, popsicle stick, vinegar, baking powder
- matches, a jug, water, plastic dropper
- red cabbage indicator (see pages 10–11)

The plan

We are going to investigate what happens when a candle is burned in a sealed jar.

Experiment 1

1 Put the candle in the base of the jar.

2 Put a few drops of water in the jar. Don't wet the wick!

3 Light the popsicle stick with a match, then use it to light the tea light.

4 When the tea light is burning well, screw the lid down on the jar.

5 When the flame has gone out, use the indicator to test the water in the jar. It should prove acidic.

What's going on?

The candle needs oxygen to burn. With the lid closed, it uses up the oxygen in the jar. When there is none left, the flame goes out. Burning produces carbon dioxide (CO_2), some of which dissolves in the water to make carbonic acid.

Experiment 2

1 Use a clean jar. Place an empty thread spool inside the jar, and put the tea light on it to raise it up.

2 Carefully spoon three teaspoons of baking powder into the jar. Keep the powder off the tea light.

3 Light a popsicle stick with a match so you can reach the wick to light the tea light. Or you could use a long match as we did.

4 Put about 10 teaspoons of vinegar into a jug and pour it very slowly onto the baking powder around the edges of the jar. Take care to avoid the tea light.

5 Watch what happens! The powder turns to foam.

What's going on?

An *invisible* gas, carbon dioxide (CO_2), forms and puts the flame out! CO_2 is heavier than air, which it *displaces* in the jar.

Jargon Buster

Carbon dioxide (CO_2) is produced by all animals, plants, fungi and microorganisms when they breathe.

Invisible Ink!

25 minutes

It's easy to send secret messages to your friends when you write them in top secret invisible ink. The secret is in the combination of lemon juice and heat from a light bulb or an iron. The heat causes a chemical change in the lemon juice and makes it appear darker on paper.

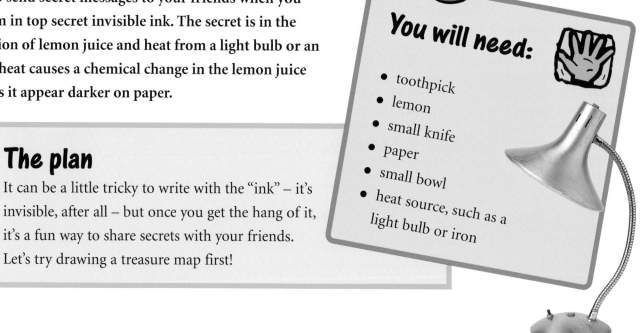

You will need:

- toothpick
- lemon
- small knife
- paper
- small bowl
- heat source, such as a light bulb or iron

The plan

It can be a little tricky to write with the "ink" – it's invisible, after all – but once you get the hang of it, it's a fun way to share secrets with your friends. Let's try drawing a treasure map first!

What to do:

1 Ask an adult to cut a lemon in half for you. Squeeze the lemon juice into a small bowl.

2 The lemon juice is your "ink!" Dip the round end of a toothpick into the bowl.

3 Draw a secret map on some paper. Use lots of lemon juice for each part you draw.

4 Allow the paper to dry until you can't see the drawing any more!

5 Now move the paper back and forth under a heat source. As the ink gets warm, your secret map is revealed.

What's going on?

The acid in the lemon juice breaks down the *cellulose* of the paper into sugars. The heat supplied tends to *caramelize* the sugars, making them brown and revealing the secret drawing.

What else can you do?

Repeat this activity with vinegar or milk to find out which makes the best invisible ink.

Density

If we took similar-sized cubes of wood and lead, the lead one would be much heavier. This is because lead is more dense than wood. It has more material packed into the same space.

You will need:

- jar, 3 drinking glasses
- various liquids and solids: syrup, cooking oil, water, grape, plastic wine cork
- blue and red food coloring
- plastic dropper, coin

The plan

We are going to compare the densities of different substances, then look at how temperature might affect density.

Experiment 1

cooking oil

water

syrup

1 Gently pour the cooking oil, syrup and water into a glass, one ingredient at a time.

2 Let the liquids settle. They should form separate layers.

3 We are going to put the grape, the coin and the cork into the jar. Where do you think they will settle?

grape in water on top of syrup

cork floats in oil

coin sinks to base of syrup

What's going on? The various substances float or sink according to their densities.

Experiment 2 Using food coloring, follow stages 1–4.

1 Take a small glass of cold water and add some drops of blue food coloring. Put it in the fridge for an hour or so.

2 Take a small glass of hot water (from the tap) and add some red food coloring.

3 Half fill a tall glass with the blue water from the fridge.

4 Use the dropper to put small amounts of the red water into the blue water. The idea is not to mix the two colors. Keep the end of the plastic dropper near the surface.

What's going on?

If you've managed to do this experiment successfully, there should be two separate layers. What do you think the position of the layers tells us about their density? Warm water is less dense than cold water, therefore the red colored water stays above the blue water in the glass.

Solid or Liquid?

Materials can exist in three states – solid, liquid and gas. Some substances can have the *characteristics* of more than one state.

You will need:

- 1 cup of cornstarch
- half a cup of water
- bowl, mixing spoon
- food coloring (just for fun)

The plan

We are going to find out how hard it is to tell a solid from a liquid!

What to do:

1 Mix together the cornstarch, the coloring and the water. It should become quite thick but still feel like a liquid.

2 Try stirring the mixture quickly and then very slowly. What happens?

Jargon Buster
Cornstarch can stand up to freezing or long cooking times!

24

3 Try to squeeze the mixture between your fingers. What happens?

4 Take some mixture in your hand and try to roll it into a ball.

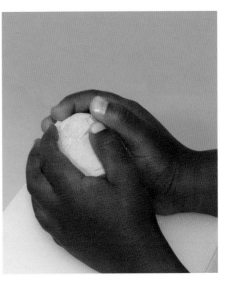

5 Put the ball down on a hard surface and hit it with your hand. (Be very careful with your hand!)

What's going on?

Cornstarch and water form a *colloid* rather than a solution. This means that the particles of cornstarch stay as a solid but are spread throughout the liquid. A colloid has unusual properties. You can stir it or let it run through your fingers like a liquid. When you try and move through it quickly (stirring fast) it resists. When you hit it, it breaks apart!

What else can you do?

Ketchup has colloid properties. What does this tell you about the best way to get it out of the bottle?

Jargon Buster
"**Colloid**" comes from the Greek word for "glue."

Making Dyes

You will need:

- an old saucepan, use of stove
- water, fork, tongs
- strips of white cotton material, (from an old pillowcase or sheet would be ideal)
- plant material, such as onion skins tea bags, turmeric, beets, acorns, walnuts, red cabbage, spinach, madder root (rubin), blackberries

The colors of objects around us are created by pigments. Some pigments are synthetic (man-made) but many occur naturally.

The plan

We are going to make dyes from different plant materials.

What to do:

1 Take one of your collected materials. We chose blackberries. Wash and mash them up with a fork.

2 Place the bits of plant in a saucepan with tap water. Put the saucepan on the stove.

3 Boil until the water is colored. Ask an adult to help you use the stove.

4 Turn off the heat. Put a piece of white cloth into the saucepan.

5 When the cloth has taken on color, just allow the saucepan to cool. Lift out the cloth using tongs.

6 Compare the dyed cloth with the original plant color.

What's going on?

Crushing and boiling destroys the plant cells and lets out the pigment. The pigment fixes itself to the cotton, which is absorbent.

What else can you do?

Try soaking or washing the cloth strips to see whether the color stays. Try out your other plants. These are the sorts of colors you might get:

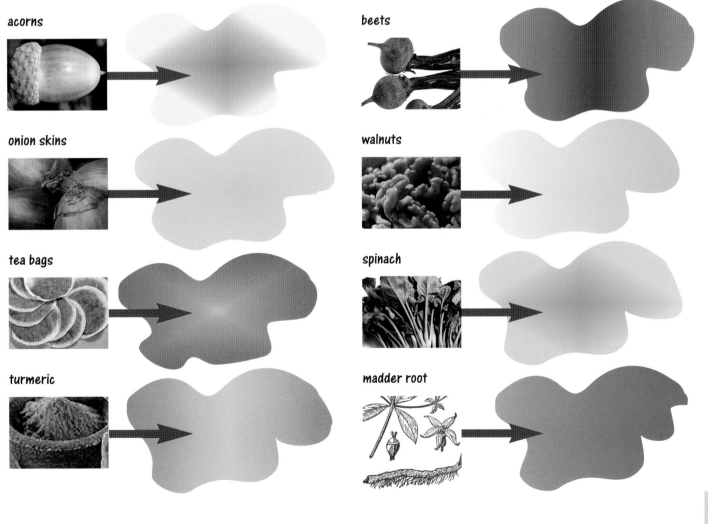

acorns

beets

onion skins

walnuts

tea bags

spinach

turmeric

madder root

Does Air Weigh Anything?

30 minutes

You will need:

- 2 balloons
- string
- scissors
- thin piece of wood, about 2 feet (600 mm) long
- balloons, marker pen

The plan

To find out if air weighs anything.

What to do:

1 Make marks about .5 inch (10 mm) from each end of the piece of wood.

2 *Suspend* the wood by a piece of string, so that it hangs horizontally. This is our weighing *balance*.

Jargon Buster
Air includes nitrogen, oxygen, argon, carbon dioxide and water vapor.

28

3 Cut two pieces of string the same length – about 6 inches (150 mm). Make a loop at the end of each piece, just big enough to slip over the wood.

4 Take two similar balloons. Blow them both up, tie off the neck of one, but let the air out of the other.

5 Tie each balloon to one of the strings.

6 Slip the strings onto the stick, exactly on the .5-inch (10 mm) marks.

What's going on?

The only difference between the two balloons is that one is "empty" and the other is full of air. But the air in the balloon is slightly compressed, so it is denser than the air around it, making the scale tip down.

What else can you do?

Try this puzzle! You'll need a kitchen scale and a glass of water. Place the glass of water on the scale. Note the weight. Now, if you put your finger into the water without touching the glass, will the weight on the scale be more or less? Answer: see below.

Answer: More, because you add the volume of water displaced by your fingers to the weight.

Magic paper?

This shocking trick depends upon materials burning at different temperatures!

You will need:

- piece of paper (taken from a notebook)
- *denatured alcohol*, salt, water
- tea light, matches
- old saucer, metal tongs

The plan

You are going to astound your friends and family by setting fire to paper without destroying it. This one needs an audience!

What to do:

1 Prepare a mixture of equal parts of denatured alcohol and water. Add a pinch of salt.

2 Place the tea light away from the solution before you light it.

3 feet (1 m)

3 Soak the paper in the solution until it is thoroughly wet.

4 Pick up the paper with the tongs and let some liquid drip off.

5 Move away from the solution, light the paper and watch it burn.

What's going on?

The denatured alcohol burns at a relatively low temperature, which is not hot enough to evaporate the water. So the paper stays wet and doesn't burn. The salt makes the flame visible. Without it, the flame would be hard to see in daylight.

Glossary

atom (A-tem) The smallest particle that makes up a chemical element.

balance (BAL-ens) A method used to compare weights of objects (see page 28).

base *(noun)* (BAYS) A substance that forms a chemical salt when combined with an acid.

basic *(adjective)* (BAY-sik) Having a base.

caramelize (KAHR-muh-lyz) To heat a sugar or syrup until it has melted and turned brown.

cellulose (SEL-yuh-lohs) Main part of plant cell walls and vegetable fibers.

characteristic (ker-ek-tuh-RIS-tik) Feature or quality of a particular person, place or thing.

colloid (KO-loyd) A gluey mixture of two substances that can behave like a liquid and a solid.

components (kum-POH-nents) Parts of something larger.

denatured alcohol (dee-NAY-churd AL-kuh-hol) A poisonous solvent, mainly ethyl alcohol (95 percent), sometimes with added coloring.

destroy (dih-STROY) To put an end to the existence of something by damaging or attacking it.

displace (dis-PLAYS) To take the place of something, to move away.

dissolve (dih-ZOLV) To become mixed into a liquid to form a solution.

evaporate (ih-VA-puh-rayt) To turn from liquid into vapor, to disappear.

glitter (GLIH-ter) Decorative plastic fragments with mirrored surfaces that add shine.

indicator (IN-duh-kay-tur) Used here to describe a liquid with known properties that reacts to an acid or a base.

invisible (in-VIH-zih-bul) Unable to be seen.

neutral (NOO-trul) In chemistry, a neutral solution is neither acidic nor basic.

permanent (PER-muh-nint) Of colors and paints: not water soluble; hard to remove.

pigment (PIG-ment) A material that changes the color of light it reflects.

suspend (suh-SPEND) To hang something, usually from string or wires.

volcano (vol-KAY-noh) An opening in the Earth's crust, which allows hot, molten rock, ash and gases to escape from below the surface.

waterproof (WAH-ter-proof) Of colors and paints: not water soluble, can't be washed out.

water-soluble (wo-ter-SOL-yuh-bul) Of colors and paints: can be washed out or dissolved with water.

Index

Web Sites

Due to the changing nature of Internet links, PowerKids Press has developed an online list of Web sites related to the subject of this book. This site is updated regularly. Please use this link to access the list:
www.powerkidslinks.com/scilab/matter/